Unlearning

The secret to better coaching engagements

Nivarti Jayaram

DASA DevOps Coach SAFe SPC PgMP PMP ACP SPS ITIL-F

Unlearning
Copyright © 2020 Nivarti Jayaram
First published in 2020

ISBN
Print: 978-0-6487911-8-8
E-book: 978-0-6487911-9-5

All rights reserved. No part of this book may be reproduced, stored in a retrieval system, or transmitted by any means (electronic, mechanical, photocopying, recording, or otherwise) without written permission from the author.

Because of the dynamic nature of the Internet, any web addresses or links contained in this book may have changed since publication and may no longer be valid. The information in this book is based on the author's experiences and opinions. The views expressed in this book are solely those of the author and do not necessarily reflect the views of the publisher; the publisher hereby disclaims any responsibility for them.

The author of this book does not dispense any form of medical, legal, financial, or technical advice either directly or indirectly. The intent of the author is solely to provide information of a general nature to help you in your quest for personal development and growth. In the event you use any of the information in this book, the author and the publisher assume no responsibility for your actions. If any form of expert assistance is required, the services of a competent professional should be sought.

Publishing information
Publishing, design, and production facilitated by Passionpreneur Publishing, A division of Passionpreneur Organization Pty Ltd, ABN: 48640637529

www.PassionpreneurPublishing.com
Melbourne, VIC | Australia

About the Author

An ICF accredited Leadership and Career Transformation Coach, Service Veteran and a UN Peacekeeper, I believe agility is a state of mind, and transformation is never a destination, but a continuous and an ongoing journey.

I promote a culture of "being dispensable" through identifying the right talent and building capability to create sustainability in organizations.

I am an expert at Enterprise Transformation, covering people, products, processes and technology, helping them to not just succeed but also thrive in the VUCA (Volatile, Uncertain, Complex, Ambiguous) world. I am passionate about people and about helping them in enhancing their self-awareness and presence so that they can identify and realize their full potential.

If you would like to know more about me, log on to:

𝒩 www.nivartijayaram.com

https://www.linkedin.com/in/nivartijayaram

Acknowledgement

THE BOOK WOULD not have been possible without constant support and prodding from my better half, Bhavana, who has been with me through all my successes and failures, always motivating me to look at my next milestone rather than just sitting on my laurels. Thanks to my sons, Kaustubhasai and Vishwas, who have been challenging and pushing me to put in all the effort needed.

A lot of the clarity in various elements mentioned in the book is an outcome of discussions with my regular travel partner Shreedevi Rao who consistently challenged by thoughts, beliefs and understanding. She has been a great friend and a travel partner.

I have to thank my esteemed colleague and friend Anu Ravi for motivating me to continue writing, overcoming writer's block and helping me understand my priorities.

Last but not the least, thanks to Akhilesh Chaturvedi, Deepti Jain, Hemanth Kotiyal, Nagini Chandramouli and Sunil Mundra who have provided their valuable thoughts and insights on their experiences with Unlearning.

Contents

Introduction ix

1	What Is Unlearning?	1
2	Learning Stages	3
3	Unlearning Stages	9
4	What to Unlearn?	13
	Skills	14
	Capabilities	15
	Competencies	17
5	Barriers to Unlearning	21
	Expertise	22
	Personal Motivation	22
	Experience	22
	Long-term Success	22
	Complexity	23
6	Facilitators for Unlearning	25
	Support System	26
	Personal Rotation	26
	Fail-Safe Environment	26
	Disruption	27

	Leadership Turnover	27
	Continuous Evaluation	29
7	Competencies Needed	31
	Presence	32
	Self-Empathy	33
	Active Listening	35
	Self-Reflection	37
	Vulnerability	38
	Emotional Agility	38
8	Framework for Unlearning	41
	DREAMS	41

Conclusion	63
Being a Coach: What to Unlearn	65
References	69

Introduction

WHAT HAVE YOU changed to be successful in the corporate world, coming from the background you are? How are you able to adapt to the new working environment? How are you managing to do so many things and still accomplish your goals? These are the questions that I am frequently asked whenever I interact closely with people and when they get to know where I come from. My answers would mostly be about how I am trained to be good at adapting to frequently changing environments – whether at work or in life, that I am a very fast learner and how I was fortunate to have found an excellent support system to help me with the initial transition period and beyond.

When I looked back and started reflecting on these questions deeper, I realized that I have been going through a process, which I could represent using the figure below:

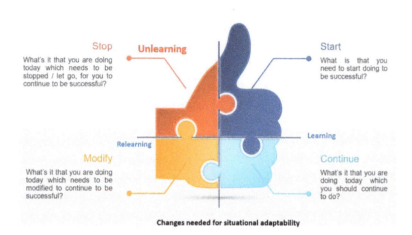

Changes needed for situational adaptability

The first three quadrants (Start, Continue and Modify) are attributed to the learning process, and the last quadrant (Stop) is what contributes to "Unlearning". I then looked at multiple scenarios that I had gone through and was fully convinced that I wouldn't have been as effective as I was, if I hadn't unlearned (stopped doing what I was not supposed to be doing), but I still wasn't clear as to what it was that I was unlearning, as I was going through the process unconsciously. What was I unlearning? I wondered. It was not skills, capabilities, competencies or behaviours but habits. On further deep diving into habits, I was exposed to the "Habit Loop", defined by Charles Duhigg in his book *The Power of Habit*. I was always "unlearning" the habits that are not suitable for the current role/environment unconsciously. This habit of unlearning has been internalized as part of the training I was put through in my initial days in the Indian Armed Forces and further through consistent practice to excel in the ever-dynamic environment we are exposed to as soldiers.

INTRODUCTION xi

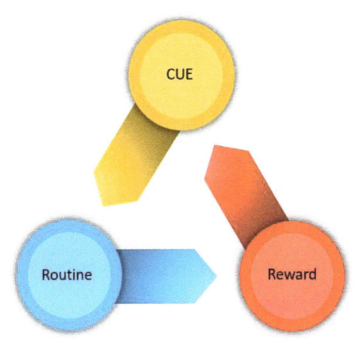

"Habit Loop" defined by Charles Duhigg in his book,
The Power of Habit

Is it always the habits that I "unlearn"? Have I been able to unintentionally "unlearn" what is needed in every scenario? The answer is "NO". There have been numerous instances wherein I had to consciously and continuously reflect on what it was that I needed to unlearn. In some cases, it was habits. In others, it was behaviours or even competencies. I used meditation techniques (Mindfulness Meditation, Yoga Nidra) and yoga to help with reflection to create greater self-awareness. In certain scenarios, even with conscious reflection, I wasn't able to figure out the "what" and had to take the help of a coach to figure it out. To reflect consistently, you need to be present fully for yourself and be in the now, which helps in raising self-awareness. Continuity and consistency are quite significant as habits/behaviours could be both conscious and unconscious. We need to continuously be available for ourselves all the time to acquire awareness of unconscious habits and behaviours. We then need to work on unlearning those if they are detrimental to our current/new environment whether at the workplace or life in general.

Transformation is the buzzword, whether it's organizational or personal. There is enormous focus on transformation across industry sectors with Digital, Agile, DevOps, Cloud transformation etc. at the organizational level. This demands continuous upskilling and exhibiting behaviours with a growth mindset at the personal level to adapt and excel.

As part of personal or organizational transformation, individuals and teams learn modern technologies, skills and behaviours and build competencies that are required for new ways of working and leading.

I have been leading organizational transformation initiatives over the past seventeen years and have been on a personal transformation journey myself – having to move across contrasting industry sectors, technologies and frameworks as part of my midlife career shift.

> Grow your talents and skills through a consistent practice and progressive learning. Learn to relearn and unlearn. Raise the bar for yourself always.
>
> —Israelmore Ayivor

INTRODUCTION

I have seen and experienced that for transformation to be complete and sustaining, while it's important to learn new skills and build capabilities and competencies in new areas, it is equally important to "Unlearn" the skills, competencies, habits and behaviours that are incompatible with the new areas/avenues.

As part of sharing my experience of transforming organizations and myself personally, I have tried to outline the need and significance of unlearning, what to unlearn, the barriers that could stop us from doing so and the facilitators that we could use to our advantage during the entire process.

Learning and unlearning must happen simultaneously and not independently for it to be more effective and efficient. For example: If you are living in countries like Britain, India, Japan and Australia – where people drive on the left side of the road – you would be used to driving a car that is a right-hand drive. If you happen to suddenly move to countries like the United States or Europe, you will concentrate on learning about the rules and regulations and familiarizing yourself with the cars that are left-hand driven. As long as you are conscious about the fact that you are now driving a left-hand driven vehicle as against the one you are used to and/or doing so in normal circumstances, everything seems to be going smooth. However, the moment there is an emergency or if you are not concentrating enough and have to react instantly, the default behaviour of a right-hand drive takes over. This is purely because the default behaviours have been developed and wired between the body and the brain due to consistent repetitive practice over a lengthy period and have become your unconscious competence.

This is one of the many examples that highlights the need to unlearn certain skills, competencies and behaviours that you have been practicing over many years while you start learning something entirely new. It doesn't mean it can't happen, but just that it may take that much more time and effort if it has to be done independent of learning.

With reference to organizational transformation as well, the coaches, change agents or champions strategize, visualize and plan for the effort involved in helping employees and customers and leadership in learning new skills, competencies and behaviours with absolute lack of focus on what needs to be unlearned.

For example: As part of the Agile Transformation initiative, we train all managers/leaders to learn and develop the attributes of practicing Servant Leadership. However, at the first sign of failure or challenge, it is seen that most leaders/managers fall back to the command-and-control style of leadership. This is because the "Unconscious Mind" takes over and brings out the behaviour that an individual has been most successful within a similar scenario or circumstance. This derails the transformation efforts put in so far and pulls the team back completely. Bringing the team back on track takes double or more the effort than it took originally due to the lack of confidence in the transformation journey.

Trying to transform organizations without understanding the current culture – and if and how it needs to be transformed for the new ways of working or leading to be successful – only results in an organization transitioning to a new state rather than transforming to a new entity. When we do focus on cultural transformation, apart from focusing on the new culture, we want the people in the organization to embark on it. It's important to identify the cultural aspects that we need to strictly do away with and not provide a fallback option to those for the transformation to sustain and thrive.

As part of my on going journey of being a coach, unlearning again came to life as I was struggling for the coaching conversations to be effective with my inbuilt behaviors and habits clouding my conversations and many a time, completely influencing my conversations and attempting to lead clients to an outcome I desired for them than themselves.

I have also brought to life certain tools, techniques and the framework that could be used for unlearning, defining each step of the framework, what would be the inputs, the exploration, ways to define action items, the need for validation/ progress measurement and reaffirm if they are still in line with the identified outcomes. It also provides for an opportunity to relook at the goals from time to time during the journey and change or realign actions as needed. The framework is aimed at making the individual self-sufficient and can be used not just in the context of Unlearning but also to change anything else in life as well.

1
What Is Unlearning?

WHILE LEARNING IS the process of acquiring new or modifying existing knowledge, behaviours, skills, values or preferences, **Unlearning** is letting go of one or more of these consciously rather than unconsciously, since losing something unconsciously takes a long time and can't be measured.

"Unlearning" as a term was coined way back in 1971 by James G. Greeno, an American educational psychologist, who defined it thus: "Unlearning has been viewed as memory elimination in a system".

Ashworth (2006) and Bennis (1976) have described unlearning as a "planned organizational change" that requires "conscious, deliberate and collaborative effort to improve the operations of a human system".

Unlearning is a "gradual, continuous process that occurs more or less simultaneously with learning. When old routines are replaced by new ones, they are gradually removed from an organization's memory" (more of an unconscious process being referred to).

Karen Becker's group adds another dimension when they claim that unlearning can occur at an individual level: "The process by which individuals and organizations acknowledge and release prior learning (including assumptions and mental frameworks) in order to accommodate new information and behaviors" (Becker, 2005).

Unlearning is often associated with keywords such as forgetting, knowledge loss and knowledge destruction. Those are also often depicted in dyads: Unlearning/learning (Akgün et al., 2003), forgetting/retaining, knowledge loss/knowledge acquisition and knowledge destruction/knowledge creation.

2
Learning Stages

Sir John Whitmore is regarded as a pioneer in the field of business coaching. Along with Tim Gallwey, Laura Whitworth and Thomas J. Leonard, he is credited with launching modern coaching in the 1970s. For some people, Sir John will always be best known as the co-creator of the GROW model, one of the most established and successful coaching models.

In his book *Coaching for Performance*, Prof Sir John Whitmore explains learning as a repetitive process undertaken consciously through a lifecycle (Fig. 1 below).

Fig. 1 Learning Cycle by John Whitmore

Stage 1
Unconscious Incompetence: *You don't know what you don't know.* This is a stage where you are not aware of even the existence of a certain skill that you need to acquire.

The question we need to ask here is – are we aware of every skillset available in the world today? Even with the current technological, communicational and social media landscape, I would say NO. Many times, I have found myself in a state of unknowing, where I don't really know or understand what it takes to manage a situation or overcome an issue at hand. That is when I am in the stage of Unconscious Incompetence.

Stage 2
Conscious Incompetence: *You know what you don't know.* This is a stage where you are aware of a certain skill that you need to acquire and are looking out for ways and means to get it.

Stage 3
Conscious Competence: *You learnt what you don't know.* This is a stage where you have learnt a certain skill that you need to acquire and are practicing it to build your capability and gain competence.

Stage 4
Unconscious Competence: *You have successfully integrated what you know.* This is a stage where you have gained a level of competence in a certain skill, so much so that it is integrated into your behaviour and has become a habit.

For example: Till five or six years ago, I didn't know that a field like professional coaching existed and that it had so much prominence. I was in a state of **Unconscious Incompetence** about professional coaching at that stage.

I came across a reference to professional coaching as I was researching about Agile Coaching and stumbled upon "Coaching Agile Teams" by Lyssa Adkins. Once I knew that professional coaching exists and had some basic idea about it from looking at the International Coach Federation (ICF), I moved from a state of **Unconscious Incompetence** to **Conscious Incompetence**.

I was very intrigued by the competencies a coach would need to develop and internalize, as advised by ICF. On reflecting, I felt I was practicing some elements of the competencies without actually being aware of them. I started looking for agencies that could help me to formally get into coaching.

I started my acquaintance with Yayati Consulting, an organization that helps with experiential learning of all aspects of coaching for individuals over a period, as advised by ICF. I went through 130 hours of experiential learning on eleven core competencies of a coach and have so far complete more than 600 hours of coaching, both pro-bono and paid. With so much of learning and practice, I can now say that I have moved from **Conscious Incompetence** to **Conscious Competence** on being a coach.

Have I reached a stage of being a coach who has internalized coaching to be his personality, which I consider is the state of being (coaching being your default behaviour state)? I would say I'm still a long way away. If and when I manage to be a coach rather than doing coaching, that is, embrace all aspects of coaching to be a part of my true authentic self, that is when I will be moving from Conscious Competence to Unconscious Competence.

Another example that everyone could relate to is driving skills.

When you don't know how to drive, you are in a state of **Conscious Incompetence**.

As you start learning how to drive, you are very conscious about where the accelerator, brake and clutch are and which gear you are in. Coordination of all the elements is quite difficult, and it's a very bumpy ride in the beginning. You start getting confident as you practice more and more, and coordination becomes easy, but you will still keep looking out for these when you are in peak traffic or driving on a hilly terrain. A certain level of competence is attained but driving is still a conscious exercise for you. You would have moved from **Conscious Incompetence** to **Conscious Competence**.

The more you continue to drive, the more you are no longer conscious about all the elements involved, and your actions and responses to different situations are automatic as driving gets fully ingrained into your habits. You are able to focus on other aspects like talking to your companions, listening to music or even attending phone calls while driving, as driving now has become your **Unconscious Competence**.

3
Unlearning Stages

UNLEARNING IS ALSO a repetitive process undertaken consciously through a lifecycle (below figure).

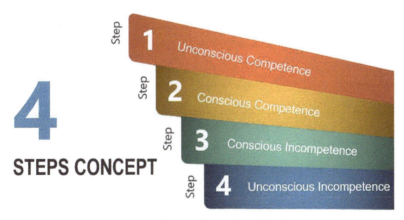

The Unlearning Cycle

Stage 1
Unconscious Competence: *You don't know what you need to unlearn.* This is a stage where you are not aware of what it is that you need to unlearn.

The questions we need to ask here are many. How much of self-awareness do you have? How well do you know and understand yourself? What is your level of consciousness around your behaviours and habits in different circumstances? What is it that you are looking to learn? What is the goal that you are looking to accomplish and why? The responses to these questions are quite significant and would define if you can go through the unlearning journey on your own or whether you need to look for support.

Stage 2
Conscious Competence: *You know what you need to unlearn.* This is a stage where you are clear about the goals that you would like to accomplish, are aware of what you need to unlearn and have figured out why. This could be the habits, behaviours, competencies, capabilities or even skills that are not aligned with your goals or new ways of working or leading.

Stage 3
Conscious Incompetence: *You have unlearnt what you need to.* This is a stage where you have started the process of unlearning what you need to. However, it's still a conscious process where you constantly introspect if there are traces of the behaviours, habits or skills that you are looking to unlearn.

Stage 4
Unconscious Incompetence: *You have successfully taken out the old habits/ behaviours/ competencies/capabilities or skills from your unconscious.* This is a stage where you no longer remember the earlier traits that you were looking to unlearn. Moving from conscious incompetence to unconscious

incompetence is the toughest part and could take a very long time. In some cases, this could never even happen, and we are left in the state of conscious incompetence. This doesn't mean that unlearning is not complete, but we need to be conscious of what we need to stop exhibiting or practicing.

4
What to Unlearn?

SKILLS, CAPABILITIES AND COMPETENCIES are often used interchangeably just like Habits and Behaviours. These are quite unique and are interrelated as well, but not synonyms of each other. Let's explore each of them.

Skills

This is an ability and capacity acquired through deliberate, systematic and sustained effort to smoothly and adaptively carry out complex activities or job functions involving ideas (cognitive skills), things (technical skills) and/or people (interpersonal skills).

Skills could be of two types:

1. Hard Skills: These are technical skills that are teachable, can be quantified and measured and are specific to a role or responsibility. These are domain specific and aligned to certain job functions.

    Examples:

    - Proficiency in a foreign language
    - Plumbing
    - Driving
    - Machine operation
    - Computer programming

2. Soft Skills: These are generic skills that are very subjective and hard to quantify. These are part of an individual's personality and define how well you operate with other people in a group, community or society.

    Examples:

    - Communication
    - Leadership

- Conflict management
- People management
- Stakeholder management

Capabilities

The ability or capacity to exhibit the skills, whether soft or hard skills, that one is trained in to achieve intended objectives defines the capability of that individual. This is defined by the length of your experience in practicing a certain skill.

In an organization, it is the ability and capacity to implement or execute its strategic objectives to achieve the intended business outcomes. This is a combination of people, technologies, processes and practices involved in an organization towards a specific intention or objective.

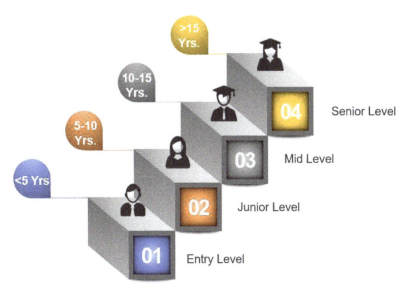

Levels of Experience

Entry Level (0–3 Years):

An entry-level position is the starting point for many careers and the first job for a college graduate or trainee in his/her chosen domain. It's a practice in large and mid-size organizations in certain domains. Work experience is often acquired through an internship program prior to employment or on-the-job training is also offered. In this position, employees work under supervision and shadow of the next-level employees to develop their understanding and are also reverse-shadowed for some time to gain confidence in the routine tasks they are expected to undertake.

Junior (4–8 Years):

Employees at this level are expected to handle their work independently or under supervision. This level needs a certain level of problem-solving skills, resourcefulness and responsibility. Work-related experience and specific skills in the domain are often expected.

Middle (9–15 Years):

Employees at this level support, motivate and assist junior and entry levels. They are deeply involved in the day-to-day operation of a business and have a comprehensive knowledge of their field of specialization. They are good at executing the strategic plans outlined by senior level leadership, provide guidance and mentorship and are expected to be the guiding light for the lesser experienced.

Senior (>15 Years):

This is considered to be the most experienced layer in an organization. People with this level of experience are able to customize, enhance and innovate on the existing product and its features to gain maximum return on investment (ROI). They usually lead and manage teams comprising members less experienced and provide guidance and mentorship and own the deliverables/outcomes of the team.

Competencies
The application of an individual's skills/capabilities to successfully and effectively achieve the intended objectives defines his/her competency. This is defined by the level of expertise in a given field/skill.

The ability of an organization to bring together all its capabilities to successfully achieve its business objectives, and the effectivity with which it is achieved, defines its competency.

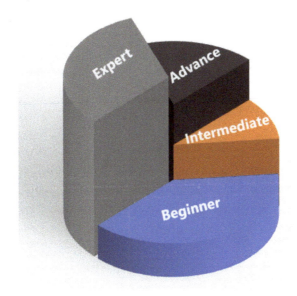

Competency Levels

Beginner:
You understand the theoretical concepts and have experience as an intern or an on-job trainee. You need mentoring and support to exhibit the skills and are under someone else's guidance.

Intermediate:
You have a good understanding of the concepts and can undertake tasks around the capability independently with minimal guidance. You still look for advice or recommendations in handling complex scenarios.

Advanced:
You have a good understanding of the concepts and can undertake tasks around the capability independently with minimal guidance. You are looked at as a go-to person by your immediate peers and team to help in handling complex scenarios. You have the ability to provide relevant ideas and perspectives on improving the capability, which can be easily be implemented. You are capable of training others in the application of the relevant competency.

Expert:
You are capable of coaching others in the application of this competency. You can provide guidance, troubleshoot and answer questions related to this field where the skill is used. You can focus on strategic aspects and have demonstrated consistent excellence in applying this competency. You are considered the go-to person in the field, both within and outside the organization, and lead the development of reference and resource materials for this competency. You

can explain the relevant process elements and issues in the simplest of terms with sufficient detail during discussions and presentations to senior leadership, to foster a greater understanding.

5
Barriers to Unlearning

AS WITH LEARNING new things in life, we would have some barriers that would stop us from unlearning too. These could be due to our self-limiting beliefs, false assumptions, failures in certain instances etc. In this chapter, we will look at those barriers that could stop us from unlearning what we want to.

Expertise:
This is one of the major barriers to unlearning. When an individual is considered an expert in a certain field or domain, there are lot expectations at superior, peer and subordinate levels within the organization, and at social levels externally – in terms of their performance and ability to contemplate/comprehend given situations and deliver. An image/brand is built up within the organization as well as in social circles, which the person feels the need to maintain. These aspects also build up the person's ego and influence his/her personality traits and behaviour.

Personal Motivation:
Lack of personal motivation could be either attributed to an individual being content with his/her lot or could be a result of people around them or the system they are working in. This could stop an individual from realizing the need to look for learning something new, as well as unlearning what is not needed.

Experience:
The level of experience you have guarantees a corresponding level of success in the area that you are working in or involved with. The outcome of this results in greater visibility, reputation, credibility and trust within the system – amongst the co-workers and leadership within the organization – enhancing your value, utility and position.

Long-Term Success:
If you have been continually successful over a long period of time, you will develop a strong belief system towards the

kind of behaviours you exhibit, the values that drive those behaviours and the habits you built in order to accomplish the success.

Complexity:
Complexity of change involved is also a big barrier to unlearning, and the level of complexity is directly proportional to the amount of resistance. The process of unlearning involves changing "Who you are?" rather than "What do you do?" This leads to a lot of questions about the person's values, belief system and underlying assumptions, and these are very complex to be aware of, accept and understand. The greater these need to be changed, the more the resistance to that change.

6
Facilitators for Unlearning

THE JOURNEY OF unlearning can become easier if we can find the right environment and support system to help us through the process. In this chapter, we will look at the facilitators that we could use to successfully complete our journey and complete our transformation as intended.

Support System:
While you may have a lot of people for company through your learning journey, as it is more external, the unlearning journey could be very lonely. Hence, it is important to identify the right people – who one can trust, confide in and are non-judgemental. The deeper the beliefs, values or assumptions that one is trying to change, the stronger the support system needed. This is where having a good coach would be of great help in succeeding through the journey.

Personal Rotation:
In an organizational context, moving people out of their current teams/roles to an entirely different role could be a great facilitator for unlearning. Even for individuals, moving to a different team/role where we lack expertise makes it quite natural and easier to unlearn. The reasons for this are the lack of expectations – both from our stakeholders and from within ourselves. Also, being in an entirely new area makes it easier to look inward to understand what we need to change in order to adapt to the environment, team members and stakeholders that we need to influence, impact and deliver to. This big change in our mindset, which moves from an inside out to outside in approach, is a significant contributor to identify the need for unlearning and for what we need to do.

Fail-Safe Environment:
Fear of failure is there in our personal and professional life and is what mostly stops us from taking up challenging work or making challenging decisions. More than fear of failure and our acceptance of it, it is the repercussions of society and the people close to us that stops us. Having a fail-safe

environment, where failure is seen more as a learning than lack of capability or potential, is crucial to unlearning. This also helps us develop a culture of innovation and experimentation in teams and organizations, which leads to developing high-performing individuals, teams and organizations.

Disruption:
Major disruptions are introduced voluntarily by organizations or mandated due to any of the following reasons:

- The way people work in an organization/team through the introduction of Agile/DevOps/Lean Transformations
- Major change in processes/guidelines being followed through the implementation of ISO/ CMMI etc.
- Introduction of new emerging technologies and products like Big Data, AI/ML, Blockchain etc.
- Major changes in the strategic direction of the organization or businesses they are involved in
- New acquisitions and integrations that bring forth major cultural differences between the acquiring and acquired organizations

Each of these disruptions demand change in our skillsets, competencies and behaviours in order to adapt and excel. For us to be successful, these force us to look for areas of improvement and new areas of learning and unlearning.

Leadership Turnover:
A change in senior leadership also changes the culture of the team and how we operate on a day-to-day basis towards

achieving the vision, goals and objectives set at a team, product, portfolio or organizational level. Sometimes, there could even be a change in vision and objectives based on the influence or direction the new leader is coming forward with. This forces us to look for ways to adapt ourselves to the changed operating model, diverse expectations, preferred communication channels etc. For us to thrive in the new world, we will need to learn, unlearn and relearn various aspects of our habits and behaviours to excel and achieve continued success.

All the above elements are external events that force us to unlearn and align to an outside in approach to unlearning, which means we look at what is changing outside and identify what we need to change in order to adapt. This could result in five different responses based on our personality, character and attitude: fight, flight, lead, adapt or be content with.

- Fight: This response is when one wants to be oneself, looks to challenge the need to change and/or tries to resist the change and wants to still be successful.
- Flight: This response is when one feels uncomfortable or overwhelmed with the change and looks for ways to move out of the team/organization to another area.
- Lead: This response is when one is proactive in being an early adopter of the change, looks at change as an opportunity to grow and becomes an influencer in making others adapt to the change as well.
- Adapt: This response is when one is looking at what needs to change to be successful in adapting to the changing environment.

- Content: This response is when one is on the fence, which means one neither adapts to the change nor resists the change. People like this are content with where they are in their lives, are not aspirational and go with the flow.

Continuous Evaluation
Continuous Evaluation is an inside out approach to change. This means the transformation is self-driven – wanting to be a better person than the previous day/ month or year – and not prompted by external events. The transformation is voluntary and not forced, and the drive to transform lasts longer and is consistent. As part of this, one is constantly validating their goals and objectives from time to time and looks for opportunities for learning, relearning and unlearning. There is a lot of focus and dependency on tools and frameworks that help in continuous evaluation, define goals and objectives and identify what to learn, unlearn and relearn. Having a coach to work through the process and partner in the evaluation process as well as continuous reflection helps in achieving the goals faster.

7
Competencies Needed

FOR US TO effectively and efficiently unlearn, we would need to develop certain competencies that help us in the process of unlearning. In this chapter, we will look at those competencies which would help us to identify what to unlearn, validate our progress from time to time and accomplish our goals and objectives:

Presence

Presence means different things to different people, based on their context and how they are looking at it. I picked up a few definitions from the famous book, *Presence – Bringing your Boldest Self to your Biggest Challenges* by Amy Cuddy. I have quoted some below:

> *Presence is removing judgement, walls, and masks so as to create true and deep connection with people or experiences.*
>
> —Pam, Washington State, USA

> *Presence is loving people around you and enjoying what you do for them*
>
> —Anonymous, Croatia

> *Presence is being myself and keeping confident, whatever happens*
>
> —Abdelghani, Morocco

Amy herself defines "presence" as the state of being attuned to and able to comfortably express our truest thoughts, feelings, values and potential. As per the author, our search for presence isn't about finding charisma or extraversion or carefully managing the impression we're making on other people. It's about the honest powerful connection that we create internally, with ourselves.

Presence, in the context of unlearning, is about how much and how well you know and understand yourself, the changing situations, your working environment and people around you. The level of presence one has — through being present to oneself, how you react/respond to changing scenarios, the working environment and people around you — helps you to improve your level of self-awareness and consciousness. This further defines how we respond/react to those situations, coupled with self-reflection, empathy, active listening and the right level of emotional agility to help us identify the need for unlearning, what to unlearn and why.

Some of the tools that are helpful in improving our presence are mindfulness meditation, yoga nidra, journaling and evaluation.

Self-Empathy
Karla McLaren in her book, *The Art of Empathy: A Complete Guide to Life's Most Essential Skill*, defines empathy as:

> "A social and emotional skill that helps us feel and understand the emotions, circumstances, intentions, thoughts, and needs of others, such that we can offer sensitive, perspective, and appropriate communication and support."

As per McLaren, empathy is also a major topic of interest in our personal and professional life, where it helps us understand others well enough to successfully communicate and work with them. It helps us connect with others and feel how they feel and understand things from their perspective, thereby making it easier for us to work with them. Empathy is fundamental to our social and emotional skills. Empathy, in general, is outward driven, which means it is always focused on people whom we are working with or have relationships with.

Self-empathy is inward driven and needs a higher level of consciousness, self-awareness and reflection. Self-empathy is the ability to understand your own emotions, your behaviours in certain circumstances, the thoughts that drive you and your own needs. It's a process of self-discovery and how much you can read, understand and relate to yourself as an individual.

It's much easier to be empathetic to others than to ourselves. Imagine a situation where you are very angry. If you need to be empathetic to yourself in that situation, you need to be aware of the fact that you are angry, be able to understand what drove your emotions, reflect on the why and be compassionate enough to address it.

Being empathetic to others need not necessarily mean you are self-empathetic too. On the contrary, most people who are empathetic to others are found to be lacking in self-empathy. To be good at self-empathy, you will need to have a very high level of emotional intelligence in order to be able to visualize, feel and understand your emotions when you are exhibiting that emotion itself. Much much easier said than done, isn't it?

You may have to travel a bumpy path to develop self-empathy as you may not always like the person you see in the mirror as you develop your levels of consciousness and discover a new you that you never knew existed. The next step is to be able to acknowledge who you are and slowly start accepting it. It's a journey, and the more you discover yourself, the deeper the connect with yourself. You cannot empathize with yourself until and unless you accept who you are and are comfortable with it.

One needs to find the right balance as being too inward looking can result in you losing connectivity to the external world, and too much focus on being empathetic to others may result in compromising self-care and self-empathy.

Building resilience, self-awareness, self-reflection and emotional intelligence will lead to better self-empathy.

Active Listening
Active listening is the ability to listen, focusing completely on the person in the conversation, understanding the message, comprehending it, looking for what is not being spoken through verbal clues, body language and energy shifts, and responding empathetically.

Extending this a step further, it is the ability to understand how the conversation is influencing us personally. The ability to comprehend our own emotions, energy shifts, mental models and our limiting beliefs that become visible is the state of actively listening to ourselves.

I define the state of listening at five levels:

Hearing (Level 1): At this level, you are just hearing a conversation and have zero presence in that moment. You wouldn't be able to recollect even a bit of the conversation at the end of it as you are in a state of ignorance and not even listening.

Listening to understand (Level 2): At this level, you are listening keenly to what is being spoken to understand it, but the state of listening is more at a literary level than emotional. Your focus is limited to understanding the meaning of the conversation.

Listening to comprehend (Level 3): At this level, you are not listening and understanding word for word but are listening to the intent behind the statements being made. This is the level where you begin to understand the emotions and thoughts behind what is being spoken.

Empathetic listening (Level 4): At this level, you are listening to the language, emotions and thoughts behind what is being spoken, the energy shifts and also changes in body language at various stages of conversation. You are able to put yourself in the shoes of the other person and feel what he/she feels.

Listening to self (Level 5): At level 4, there is a countertransference of emotions, feelings and energy from the person in the conversation to you. The highest level of listening is when you can listen to yourself completely to understand how you are feeling, your own emotions, your thoughts, where they are headed etc. When you are in this high state of awareness, you will always find a lot of hidden aspects of your own personality and character, which are normally invisible.

Self-awareness and the emotional intelligence levels of an individual define which state of listening you are at and influence the strength of your relationships with others and yourself.

Self-Reflection
Self-reflection is the ability to examine, introspect your behaviours in various circumstances, the emotions you exhibited, your values and beliefs, the triggers that drove those behaviours, the thoughts that arise due to the various events happening around you and the impact they have on yourself.

Self-reflection is a great skill to continuously evolve your understanding of who you are and what is impacting and influencing you at a given point in time. This helps in building your state of self-awareness and consciousness, making it possible to define who you want to be.

Once you define your goals of who you want to be and identify what you will need to change in order to get there, this skill helps you to track and validate your progress towards the new you.

Self-reflection is a way to make lots of small course corrections away from less desirable thoughts and behaviours towards those that promote greater emotional well-being through enhanced levels of emotional intelligence.

The benefits of self-reflection are improved self-awareness, knowing why you do what you do, awareness of your values and beliefs (both positive and self-limiting), reduced stress and anxiety and a positive outlook to life.

Vulnerability
Vulnerability is the ability to express your thoughts, emotions, feelings and your strengths and weaknesses in any group without the fear of being judged. It comes from a state of high clarity, understanding and acceptance of who you are. It is the ability to say, "I don't know what this is, or I don't really understand how to deal with the situation", to anyone you are interacting with.

It's about putting yourself in a position where you can be undermined or rejected. It's about admitting that you are bad at some things and taking responsibility without blaming others.

Brene Brown in her book *Daring Greatly* says a person who can make themselves vulnerable, exposing their weaknesses without any regard to what others thinks, is saying to the world, "This is who I am and it doesn't matter what you think of me who I am".

Emotional Agility
As per Susan David in her book *Emotional Agility*, she defines it as being flexible with your thoughts and feelings so that you can respond optimally to everyday situations. Yet, it's not about controlling your thoughts or forcing yourself into thinking more positively. It's about choosing how you respond to your emotional warning system.

Emotional agility is about the ability to identify the thinking, behaviour patterns and habits of the mind and body that can stop us from realizing our full potential, and ensuring we don't continue to react/respond in the same old way to similar, new or different situations in life.

People with high levels of emotional agility are continuously evolving their personality, character and behavioural traits, which helps them to be successful in the dynamic VUCA world. They are able to overcome stressful situations much more easily and endure setbacks by being flexible, resilient, open and growth-minded.

They too are faced with anger, disappointment, sadness, stress and negativity, but their progressive approach to life and their growth mindset help them overcome these with their focus being on long-term success rather than short-term gains.

8
Framework for Unlearning

Dreams are which the mind conceives, heart desires, and the soul believes.

—*Unknown*

D R E A M S

1. Introduction
THIS SECTION DESCRIBES a self-coaching process that involves six steps (Discover, Refine, Evaluate, Action, Measure and Synchronize) as a systematic methodology for Unlearning. This coaching model provides a structured approach to identify what to unlearn, and how to measure and evaluate coaching results. The model is predominantly created to follow the full coaching lifecycle for an individual, where the person spends dedicated time with full commitment and availability. These steps simulate the way ICF describes coaching and its

partnering process with clients in a thought-provoking and creative style that empowers them to realize their full potential, which enables them to accomplish the results they want.

The DREAMS model takes account of a person's

- Perceptions, beliefs and views
- Habits and behaviours, which may have yielded results in the past but are no longer yielding the desired or expected results
- Limiting beliefs and the paradox trap
- Validates his/her assumptions and challenges his/her commitment to the agreed actions
- The emotional status of the person, which has created the barriers to move ahead or resulted in him/her being trapped

The experiences and research suggest that the above points contribute to

i. The creation of stumbling blocks for any individual
ii. The creation of blind spots that impact productivity, relationships, effectiveness and outcomes

The DREAMS model considers these behavioural, habitual and emotional traits and highlights those that one needs to stop focusing on. It does so by creating awareness about the need for unlearning and reflection, and the need to empathize with oneself and commit one's wilful acceptance in his/her unlearning journey.

The DREAMS model empowers an individual to become self-sufficient and provides a framework through which he/she can coach themselves to work through situations/current reality and adopt the required changes to continuously enhance their boundaries to realize their full potential.

The DREAMS model is very simple to practice; it is non-judgemental and very effective. It also empowers the individual to build his/her ability to self-introspect and reflect, build self-esteem, have confidence in his/her abilities and realize his/her true potential.

2. **The Self-Coaching Process**
The following are the distinct phases of the coaching model as depicted in the figure below:

2.1 D – Discover

Self-coaching involves active communication between the individual wanting to coach themselves, and additional key stakeholders who can provide significant inputs on the person's personality, habits, behaviour patterns etc. Identifying the right stakeholders who can provide honest, open and transparent feedback is key to a successful transformational journey. This is because if you want to transform, it is imperative to understand who you are today, and only then can you decide who you want to be. An effective and in-depth discovery phase is foundational to successful transformation, whether at an individual level or in an organizational context.

Many things happen at this point. They are explained below:

- Clarity on the need for transformation and commitment to embark on the transformation journey.
- Identification of key stakeholders who can provide honest, open and transparent feedback. The stakeholders should be those whom the individual looking to transform completely trusts and can confide in. It's important to focus on people who can provide feedback on both positive and negative elements, more so on negative aspects as that's what we are looking to stop, modify or change.
- Establish objectives and specific goals for the transformation journey and further share those with the stakeholders on setting expectations, timelines, ground rules and the alignment of goals and objectives.

- Sharing goals and objectives with all the stakeholders is again a significant step for the success of a self-coaching initiative. This serves two purposes:
  o Creates a baseline from where you can seek continuous feedback to validate progress being made. A high level of consciousness and awareness is needed if we have to evaluate our progress ourselves, and it takes a long time to reach there; hence the continuous evaluation and feedback is essential.
  o Creates a sense of social pressure which helps us to be on our transformation journey if we do wander/deviate from it.

Competencies Used: Stakeholder Management, Strategic Vision.

Objective:

- Defining the need for transformation, what it is that we need to start learning new, modify, relearn and unlearn.
- Explore the goals and objectives the individual is looking to accomplish and the importance of those.
- Understand current realities that the person is aware of and the known ways he/she intends to move forward.
- To get a perspective and view of what others think and feel about an individual.
- Understand his/her current assumptions, beliefs, values and behaviours, which means the overall emotional state.

- Understand strengths, constraints and limitations within which one is currently operating.
- To bring alive the blind spots and hidden strengths that would not have been noticed or observed.

Input:

- Behavioural, leadership approach and personal attributes collected from stakeholders through a series of questions, a set of people who consist of personal relations, reporting managers, peers and reporting team members.

Process:

- In the first session, reflect on why you are looking to transform, what is driving the need for transformation and clearly state the understanding of your current situation.
- Identify key stakeholders for evaluation and kick off the evaluation process:
  o List out at least four stakeholders from each of the groups below:
    - Whom you look up to and are greatly influenced by
    - Your peers at your workplace or people who you are great friends with
    - Your next level at your workplace
    - The lowest person in the hierarchy
  o The evaluation process consists of 360-degree feedback, which must be conducted to create a

FRAMEWORK FOR UNLEARNING

baseline of the current state from a people perspective. The process should be completed well in advance, before the first session.
o Once the feedback is received, the data should be compiled and evaluated by the individual seeking the feedback.
o A slot of thirty minutes per person, identified for the 360-degree feedback should be kept aside for discussion/clarification on the feedback.
o The individual should neither challenge the feedback given nor provide any justification for any elements provided in it.
o Essentially, the feedback falls into one of the four quadrants below:
- Realized Elements: These are the aspects of your personality, values, beliefs, habits or behaviours that you think you exhibit in your day-to-day life and your stakeholders also recognize.

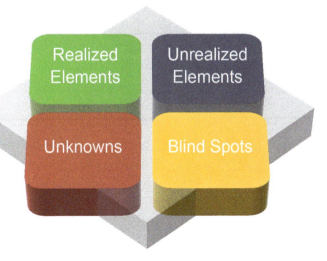

- Unrealized Elements: These are the aspects of your personality, values, beliefs, habits or behaviours that you think you exhibit in your day-to-day life, but your stakeholders don't recognize. This means that these are patterns you think you have, but you are not exhibiting them enough for others to take cognizance.
- Blind Spots: These are the aspects of your personality, values, beliefs, habits or behaviours that you think you are not aware that you exhibit in your day-to-day life, but your stakeholders recognize. This means these are patterns you think you don't have, but you are exhibiting them enough for others to take cognizance.
- Unknowns: These are unknown unknowns, which neither you nor your stakeholders are aware of.

Outcome:

- The data will give fair access into what others around think and feel, especially those who are in the sphere of their influence and impact.
- There are valuable insights in terms of what one is good at, his/her positive traits, what he/she needs to do differently.
- The person will use the feedback and shared understanding of the current situation to identify goals and objectives, identify what to learn, relearn and unlearn, and draw a plan of action to work on diverse options to move from the current situation, behaviours, habits and attitudes.

Competencies Used: Establishing Trust, Presence, Active Listening, Powerful Questioning and Emotional Intelligence.

2.2 R – REFINE

Objective:

- Refine the goals finalized as part of the discovery phase to get certainty on what needs to be accomplished.
- Clearly outline what would change for you as part of the transformation journey and how your stakeholders can visualize the change and validate the extent of change.
- Commit to the goals and objectives with full clarity of mind.

The overall objective of this phase is to begin with the end in mind – what you want to accomplish and what is the coaching structure available to take you through the journey towards your goals and objectives.

Input:

- The data related to goal setting and summary captured based on personal reflections and stakeholder feedback during the first session.
- The enhanced understanding of realized and unrealized aspects and blind spots in diverse aspects of your life.
- You engage with the relevant stakeholders in the session and engage them in conversation to take them

through your goals and objectives, how you intend to achieve them and your expectations of continuous validation and feedback from them.

Process:

- Once you have refined your goals and objectives, you would explain to all stakeholders:
  o Why the goals and objectives you have set for yourself matter most to you at this time.
  o Why it is important for you to act on accomplishing these now.
  o What you plan to learn, relearn and unlearn in your journey of accomplishing the outcomes.
  o What the duration of your transformation journey is.
  o How you expect the stakeholders to validate your progress and provide feedback.
- You will go through a process of
  o **Mining** – Mine from the key areas of your life a list of needs, wants, be, do and haves of life.
  o **Refining** – The most critical areas from the mining data are segregated from "important" and "least critical areas" of life.
  o **Defining** – The most critical areas are converted into well-defined goals.
- Answers the need for the transformation or accomplishment of the outcomes clearly and the aspects that are driving the need.
- Answer clearly on what would change for you once you achieve the intended outcomes.

Outcome:

- An increased level of self-awareness about your current state and the strength of your relationship with your stakeholders.
- You gain the confidence of stakeholder support in your journey to evolve, grow and develop.
- You will also realize that the stakeholders are your partners in the journey, and, with their support, what was not possible before can be achieved now and in the future.
- Arrive at three inspiring goals from 15 to 25 or more listed areas across the areas of life on which you will work during the defined period.
- Your reflection during the process will bring forth a lot of insights about what is most important to you, what you value, where you may get stuck during the journey and whom you can look up to for support.

Competencies Used: Presence, Active Listening, Powerful Questioning, Self-Reflection, Designing Actions and Stakeholder Expectations.

2.3 Evaluate

Objective:

- Understand decision-making, behaviour patterns, learning styles and ability to and ways you adopt to let go, your values, beliefs, strengths and limiting beliefs relating to people with whom you interact, the inner capacities involving confidence and self-esteem.

- To help you gain awareness about your motivating factors and evaluate multiple options to finalize the most feasible ones.
- To formulate strategies as they help create the blueprint of the roadmap and milestones involved in the journey.

Input:

- The finding of the Psychometric Assessment/Profile and analysis of the 360-degree feedbacks received.
- Formulation of your strategies based on your own reflections and discussions with relevant stakeholders (mostly those you are influenced by).
- Your goals and objectives, measure of your progress and validation by your stakeholder and their feedback.

Process:

- Use objective means and a self-discovery process to help you understand your potential better and identify the elements that need to be kept intact or honed further.
- Evaluate and identify areas that need to be modified or improved further and those to be developed or acquired newly to gain the habits and attributes that can support you in accomplishing these goals.
- Identify aspects that need to be unlearned to accomplish complete transformation, which ensures you don't fall back on old habits and behaviour patterns that are detrimental to the future you.

FRAMEWORK FOR UNLEARNING

- Validate the feedback provided by the diverse stakeholders as part of the 360-degree feedbacks using Johari Window to come up with hidden strengths and blind spots.
- You will also formulate strategies based on your interactions with the relevant stakeholders. Strategies are long-term plans or blueprints that help you concentrate efforts in achieving goals. They are a series of steps that make it clear to you to
  o Provide a more practical understanding how each goal can be achieved.
  o Ensure that you work to achieve the goals with support outlined from your stakeholders.
  o Provide an insight about the importance of commitment to the actions for achieving the goals outlined and not about simply carrying out a series of actions.
  o Reduce the chances of you becoming overwhelmed and look to take one step at a time.
  o A high-level set of milestones that provide objectivity and give the journey the desired shape and progress.
  o Consciously avoid doing things the way you are habituated to do.
  o Improve the quality of your thinking and enhance your self-awareness.

Competencies Used: Presence, Active Listening, Powerful Questioning and Self-Awareness.

2.4 A – Actions
This phase is the most significant part. Your definition of actions and commitment to fulfil those will help you make

progress towards achieving the goals. After designing actions along with the relevant stakeholders, you should make all efforts in ensuring you complete those between sessions as committed.

Objective:

- To design actions – In each session formulate the action for the next one week or two weeks based on the duration you decided.
- To get into action – You take actions between two sessions on the various strategies.
- To review action – You evaluate the actions and effectiveness of those actions in discussions with the relevant stakeholders to validate progress.
- To set course correction – If there are any deviations or you are feeling resistance to act, you should reinforce the significance of those actions in discussions with the relevant stakeholders to remove the blocks and commit to continue to move forward.

Input:

- Design actions – Share detailed actions based on the strategies arrived at and outline the outcome of those actions. You share the plan of action at predefined intervals with you and the stakeholders recording them separately.
- Action attributes – Reinforcement, reassurance for yourself, validation and recognition by the stakeholders.

- Actions report – Discussion between the sessions with all the relevant stakeholders.
- Review actions – You along with the stakeholders review the action taken, between sessions.
- Course correction – You look for any deviations or resistance within, reorient yourself and set due course correction.

Process:

- You share the significance of taking actions and highlight your commitment in the journey towards accomplishing the goals you set.
- Explore any possible constraints or obstructions coming in the way of the actions outlined and ways in which you would overcome them or work around them.
- Between the sessions, you undertake the actions while continuing with your routines and priorities of daily life. While taking actions, you consistently reflect and observe the
  o intrapersonal shifts and turmoil,
  o interpersonal responses and reactions of people around you and
  o situation or context dynamics.
- You review the actions taken between sessions by diagnosing, clarifying and reflecting on various aspects such as facts, emotions, learning, implications, new goals/tasks and documenting them.
- You take stock from the previous steps of any deviations or resistance faced that stopped you from taking

an action, reflect, reinforce and remove blocks to move forward to accomplish the actions outlined.

Outcome:

- You get clarity on the why, what and how of taking actions during the journey towards the goals.
- You understand the focus needed on the purpose and timeframe of actions.
- Have clarity on the why, the actions outlined and the possibilities of accomplishing the goals outlined. This will make you enthusiastic and build your earnest desire to fulfil the actions.

Competencies Used: Managing Progress and Accountability.

2.5 M – Measure

You will experience unlearning, learning and relearning during your journey towards goals, and it is important to measure the progress from time to time to validate if it is commensurate with the amount of efforts put in.

Objective

- To measure progress made by you with reference to your identified goals, both intermediate and long-term.
- To reassure that the unwarranted habits and behaviours for accomplishing the future objectives have been let go of, or are in the process of being let go. The general tendency of us humans is that the unwarranted

aspects show up when we are under extreme pressure or in crisis situations.
- To validate if the actions are effective, are efficient and are producing the results in proportion.
- To reinforce your belief in your skills, capabilities, habits and behaviours that are already being exhibited.
- To reassure that the new behaviours developed will support you both in the present and future and will evaporate any self-doubt created.
- To review and identify best practices that have helped you in the past but were forgotten in between. Through the revival process – either through retrieving from memory or consciously becoming aware of the benefits of these practices – you revive and apply these in your life in the present context.

Input:

- List of action items identified during the earlier phase of discussions with the relevant stakeholders.
- List of milestones committed by you with the stakeholders during the goal setting.
- Hidden strengths and blind spots identified during the earlier discussions using Johari Window.
- Feedback given by all stakeholders in the mining process of goal setting in the envisioning phase.

Process:

- During the session, you explore and acknowledge progress made towards goals and validate your

commitment and the effectiveness of actions in an informal setting. You will reflect on
- current outcomes and realities,
- exploring possibilities on what to unlearn, learn and relearn,
- validating goals and
- any new insights revealed.

You capture these as information and insights and, in turn, these enhance your awareness and consciousness about who you are and how you are progressing towards who you want to be.

Outcome:

You are able to

- Identify behaviours that are detrimental and need to be eliminated in future to continue your forward movement towards your goals (unlearn).
- Identify behaviours and actions that are resulting in positive outcomes and will continue to exhibit those in future (continue).
- Understand your support system that is currently helping on your journey and on whom you can rely on for your future needs.
- Understand if you can work on blind spots, overcome deep fears and develop an abundance mentality.
- Take advantage of the hidden strengths highlighted during the feedbacks and create newer possibilities.

Competencies Used: Self-reflection, Validation and Accountability.

2.6 S – Synchronize

This is the final phase of the coaching cycle. This is where you get to review and reflect on the whole experience of the framework and its effective functioning. You review your ability to reuse the framework for all your future needs. You now have a model that helps you to be self-sufficient and not depend on a coach to unlearn, relearn and learn so as to set and accomplish goals in the future.

Objective:

To review

- The DREAMS Coaching Framework
- Strategies
- Successful behaviours
- Significant actions
- Support system
- Goals completion
- Acknowledgement for the effort
- Feedback and your report on the process, journey and accomplishment of goals
- Your summary report on the journey, progress and self-sufficiency.

Input:

- Coaching formula
- Strategies adopted

- Significant actions taken
- Goals accomplished
- Feedback reports by all the stakeholders
- Acknowledgement recorded in the prescribed format

Process:

- In the final phase of coaching, you will review the entire process, journey and accomplishment of goals.
- This is done by sharing findings, observations, acknowledgements and recommendations through a formal report.
- Acknowledgement, feedback and the road ahead.

You will exchange your findings, perceptions and views with all stakeholders on

- What has been the experience through the coaching journey.
- Where you are now in comparison to the time you set out for the journey.
- What have been the learnings and key takeaways.
- Is there anything that remains unattended or unfulfilled.
- What, if done better could have resulted in a more fruitful outcome.
- You will also give a feedback on
  o Where you finished in relation to the goal.
  o What is the confidence level you have on applying the coaching framework for your future needs.

Outcome:

- You get a structured, self-directed, self-driven, solution-focused and positive method of achieving your future goals.
- You get clarity on your successful behaviours, those you need to stop, your support system and sense of accomplishment, based on what the coachee experienced.
- The coachee and the coach get the time and space to take stock of the process, journey and accomplishment and complete anything that was not addressed.
- You are inspired and motivated by the genuine and positive acknowledgement and feedback from your stakeholders.
- Through the stakeholder feedback, you will realize the percentage of goal accomplishment.

Competencies Used: Self-Reflection, Accountability, Direct Communication and Self-Awareness.

Conclusion

Change is the only constant in the VUCA world and is the new normal. For you to adapt to the change dynamically and continue to excel, you should not just be focusing on learning new skills but extend your horizons to review and reflect on your competencies, habits and behaviours.

Understanding the various aspects of personality and character that need to evolve, aspects that no longer would be needed or those that could pull you back to your earlier state, is imperative.

Unlearning those elements of your skills, competencies, habits and behaviours that would be detrimental in the changed environment, and learning new aspects in life will help you not just survive but thrive in the dynamic and fast-paced world.

As you progress and evolve as an individual, your level of self-awareness and consciousness changes, revealing newer elements of yourself till you reach the state of super-consciousness. This essentially means the process of unlearning, learning and relearning is a journey without a destination, and the only one you should compare yourself to understand how you can be better tomorrow is "YOU".

Complete transformation of an individual cannot be achieved through just learning new aspects, because your learning is never complete without UNLEARNING.

Any journey that we undertake involves lot of self-discovery and our intent to overcome the gaps or deficiencies that are highlighted due to the enhanced state of self-awareness and self-consciousness.

Being a Coach: What to Unlearn

The journey of being is a coach is the toughest of all the journeys that I have been pursuing for the past many years and will continue to do so. International Coaching Federation (ICF) highlights the competencies listed below in addition to following ethical guidelines and professional standards and establishing a coaching agreement if you want to be a coach:

- Establishing Trust and Intimacy: Creating a safe supportive environment that produces ongoing mutual respect and trust.
- Coaching Presence: Being fully conscious and creating spontaneous relationships with clients, while employing a style that is open, flexible and confident.
- Active Listening: Focusing completely on what the client is saying and is not saying, understanding the meaning of what is said in the context of the client's desires and supporting client self-expression.

- **Powerful Questioning:** Asking questions that reveal the information needed for maximum benefit to the coaching relationship and the client.
- **Creating Awareness:** Integrating and accurately evaluating multiple sources of information and making interpretations that help the client to gain awareness and thereby achieve agreed-upon results.
- **Designing Actions:** Creating opportunities with the client for ongoing learning, during coaching and in work/life situations, and taking new actions that will most effectively lead to agreed-upon coaching results.
- **Planning and Goal Setting:** Developing and maintaining an effective coaching plan with the client.
- **Managing Progress and Accountability:** Paying attention to what is important for the client and giving responsibility to the client to take action.

While it is important for us to build the above competencies, we will now look at the aspects that we need to unlearn for us to be able to accomplish the journey of "being a coach":

- **Being Judgemental:** The environment where we are born, brought up and are leading our lives (professionally and personally) influences the level to which we judge everything around us, including people. Our ability to coach is clouded by perceptions about the coachee during the coaching conversation if we have this mindset.

    This would make us ask leading questions and drive the coachee towards an outcome that we want them to achieve because of the perceptions we have created about them and/or their situation.

BEING A COACH: WHAT TO UNLEARN

- Being Judged: I believe everyone in this world is coachable. If we find someone to be not coachable, then possibly we are not the right coach for that person. Fear of being judged as a bad coach or individual can lead us to disaster. Our desire to be liked by the person we are coaching will prevent us from challenging the person and also the ability to get to the "Who". Coaching then becomes a very transactional conversation rather than being transformational.
- Being Solution-Minded: From our early childhood, we all have been trained and mentored to develop a solution mindset. For every problem or issue that is happening around the world that comes to our notice, the first thing the mind thinks about is – what could be the possible solution from our perspective.

  We never even pause for a moment to realize whether we understand the context of the problem or the issue, the drivers, the background, the circumstances or the people involved which have resulted in that problem originating in the first place.

  If we go with the same mindset into a coaching conversation with a client, we end up giving a solution without even getting to the bottom of the core problem that the client is bringing up or understand the drivers for the goal they want to accomplish.
- Being Self-Oriented: A coaching conversation is never about how good a coach you are or what you have accomplished in your career or life. If you are focused on proving yourself to be the most capable and accomplished person involved in a coaching conversation, you will never be able to build trust and intimacy with

the client. Building trust is paramount for the client to be able to present themselves honestly and be vulnerable during conversations.
- Telling More, Asking Less: Coaching conversation is not a debate competition and should be focused on creating new insights and awareness and more "AHA" moments for the client. The coach is expected to be contributing only to 20 percent of the whole coaching conversation, which essentially means we should focus on direct, crisp and sharp communication.
- Always Ask the Right Questions: The focus should be on being present in the conversation rather than thinking about the right question to ask while the conversation is happening. I have been through the experience of losing out on important elements of the conversation by trying to either pre-empt a question to ask or be focused on the most powerful question to follow up the conversation with. This is why it is important to enhance our levels of listening and let our intuition take over to come up with questions.

The above is not an exhaustive list but still, it should give us a good starting point to accomplish our state of being a coach than just focusing on the coaching process to be followed.

References

Brown, Brene. *Daring Greatly.*

Cuddy, Amy. *Presence: Bringing Your Boldest Self to Your Biggest Challenges.*

David, Susan. *Emotional Agility.*

Duhigg, Charles. *The Power of Habit.*

McLaren, Karla. *The Art of Empathy: A Complete Guide to Life's Most Essential Skill.*

Whitmore, Sir John. *Coaching for Performance.*

Research paper by Lague, Eric & Rhaiem, Khalil. A practical approach to organizational unlearning.

www.ingramcontent.com/pod-product-compliance
Lightning Source LLC
LaVergne TN
LVHW061200281224
800074LV00050B/2784